Sunrise Book

All Times Children's Stories

Best Loved Stories

Preface

Welcome to the wonderful world of imagination - of magic, of adventure, of animals that speak, of happenings that are strange and marvellous! This is a series of five books, carefully graded with regard to language and concept. The stories have been adapted from a wide variety of sources - the Panchatantra, Aesop's Fables, the Brothers Grimm, Hans Christian Anderson and folk tales from all over the world. Colourful illustrations bring alive the characters.

We hope that through these books, children will discover the matchless pleasure of reading and will embark on a fascinating journey of discovery and delight.

Contents

SUNRISE PUBLISHERS

32/33A, Street No. 9, Bhikam Singh Colony, Vishwas Nagar, Shahdara, Delhi - 110032 (India)

Tel : +91-11-71218130, Whatsapp No. : +91-7835078000

E-mail : sunrisepub@gmail.com, export@sunrisepublisher.com

Visit us : www.sunrisepublisher.com

ISBN : 978-81-781305-0-7

Printed by **Tan Prints (India) Pvt. Ltd.**, Village Rohad, Distt. Jhajjar, Haryana

1. The Five Chinese Brothers

Once there were five Chinese brothers. They all looked exactly alike and lived happily with their mother in a little village in China. However, they were not ordinary people because the eldest Chinese Brother could swallow the sea in one gulp. The Second Chinese Brother had a neck made of rubber. The third one had a neck made of iron. The fourth could breathe under water and the youngest Chinese Brother was the strangest of all - he felt cold when it was hot and felt hot when it was cold!

Now the First Chinese Brother (who could swallow the sea in one gulp) used to go fishing. He used to swallow the sea, hold his breath, and catch as many fish as he could. Then he used to release his breath and return the sea to its place. He used to sell the fish. The whole family lived happily on his earnings.

One day the little boy who lived next door said, 'First Chinese Brother, please let me go fishing with you.' But the First Chinese Brother said, 'Oh no, you're a naughty boy. You don't listen to your mother and you won't listen to me. I will not take you with me.'

The little boy said, 'Please Chinese Brother, please take me with you. I promise I'll listen to you.'

`Very well,' said the First Chinese Brother. 'But remember, the moment I wave to you to come to me, you must immediately come to me or else you'll drown.'

'I promise! I promise!' cried the little boy.

They set off for the sea. The First Chinese Brother swallowed it in one gulp. The little boy was terribly excited. He ran to the bed of the sea shouting with delight. Never had he seen such beautiful fish or such rare shells! He began picking up all the things that caught his fancy. Soon the First Chinese Brother got tired of holding his breath. He waved to the little boy to come back but the little boy did not come back. He ran further into the sea-bed. The First Chinese Brother waved again but the naughty little boy did not listen. The First Chinese Brother could no longer hold his breath. He opened his mouth to breathe. Out rushed the sea and the little boy was drowned.

The little boy's mother was very angry. 'You've drowned my little boy, you wicked Chinese Brother,' she said.

The First Chinese Brother tried to explain but it was of no use. She did not listen. She complained to the Emperor. The Emperor's soldiers arrested him and took him to the court. The Emperor ordered him to be put to death by hanging.

When he was put in prison, the guards said to the First Chinese Brother, `Do you have a last wish?' Yes; said the First Chinese Brother. 'I want to say good-bye to my mother.'

`Very well,' said the guards. 'But mind, be here at 6 o'clock because at 7o'clock you have to die.' So the First Chinese Brother went home and sent the Second Chinese Brother (who had a neck made of rubber). Nobody noticed this because the Chinese Brothers looked exactly alike.

At 7 o'clock the judge came. The hangman put the rope round the Second Chinese Brother's neck and pulled it. But his neck stretched and s-t-r-e-t-c-h-e-d and nothing happened to the Chinese Brother.

`This has never happened before,' said the judge in surprise. `Tomorrow we'll have to chop his head off with an axe.'

Now back in prison the Second Chinese Brother said to the guards, 'Can I go home and say good-bye to my mother?'

`But you said good-bye yesterday,' said the guards.

`Oh please, let me go,' said the Second Chinese Brother.

`Very well,' said the guards. 'But mind, be back at 6 o'clock because at 7 o'clock you have to die.'

So the Second Chinese Brother went back home and sent the Third Chinese Brother (the one with the iron neck). No one noticed the change because the Chinese Brothers looked exactly alike.

At 7 o'clock the judge came. The guard put the Third Chinese Brother's head on a stone and the hangman hit hard with his axe. The axe broke into two but the Chinese Brother was unharmed.

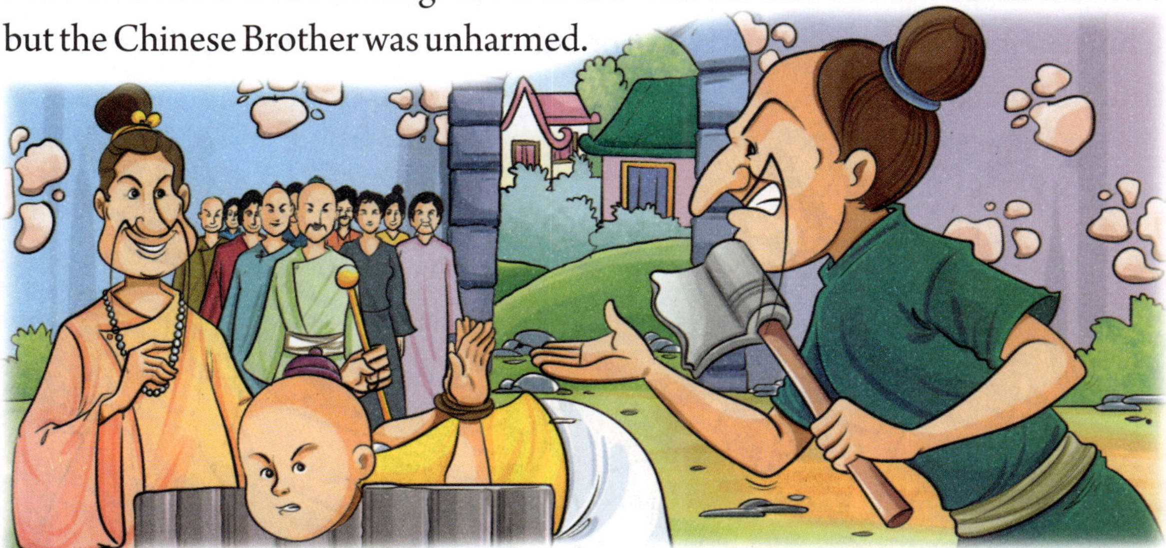

`This has never happened before,' said the judge in surprise. 'Tomorrow we'll drown him.'

Now the Third Chinese Brother persuaded the guards to let him go home and say good-bye to his mother. He now sent the Fourth Chinese Brother (the one who could breathe underwater).

At 7 o'clock they tied big stones to the hands and feet of the Fourth Chinese Brother and flung him into the sea. In the evening when they pulled him out they saw that he was alive and well.

`This has never happened before,' cried the judge. `Tomorrow we'll burn him.'

Once again the Chinese Brother persuaded the guards to let him go home to say good-bye to his mother. This time he sent the Fifth Chinese Brother (the one who felt hot when it was cold and cold when it was hot).

A very big pit was prepared. It was filled with huge logs and a great fire was lit. At 7 o'clock the Chinese Brother was flung into the fire. The whole day the fire burnt and when the logs were reduced to ashes they saw the Chinese Brother alive and well. He was shivering with cold and his teeth were chattering!

'This has never happened before,' began the judge. But the Emperor who had heard all what had happened came there and stopped him.

`You've tried to hang him, you've tried to cut off his head, you've tried to drown him and you've tried to burn him. Nothing happened. This means the Chinese Brother is innocent.' He turned to the Chinese Brother. 'I'm sorry for troubling you,' he said. He gave him a bag of gold for his troubles.

The Fifth Chinese Brother went home happily and all the five clever Chinese Brothers who helped each other lived happily ever after with their mother.

2. Mother Frost

Once upon a time there was a woman who had two daughters. One was lazy, ugly and selfish, yet she loved her because she was her own daughter. The other one was hard-working, kind and beautiful but she did not love her because she was her step-daughter. She made her do all the work of the house.

One day, while she was spinning, the step-daughter happened to prick her finger with the spindle. She went to the river to wash off her blood and her spindle fell into the river. She ran to her step-mother and said, 'Mother, my spindle has fallen into the river.'

`What!' cried the step-mother. 'Then jump into the river and get it back.'

So the poor step-daughter jumped into the river. She thought that she would drown but imagine her surprise when she found herself in a beautiful green meadow. She couldn't believe her eyes. She decided to ask someone her way home.

She had not gone far when she saw an apple tree. Its branches were laden with apples.

`Shake me! Shake me!' cried the apple tree.

'Indeed I will,' said the girl.

She shook the tree so that the apples fell. Then she made a neat pile of the apples and walked on. Now she came to an oven where cakes were being baked.

`Take us out! Take us out!' cried the cakes.

`Indeed I will,' said the girl.

She took the cakes out and then walked on.

She now came to a house where there lived a very old woman. `Will you work for me?' she asked.

`Indeed I will,' said the girl.

Then the old woman said, 'You must take care to make my bed well. Shake it so that the feathers fly about. Then children on earth will say that it's snowing. For you see, I am Mother Frost.'

So the girl began to work for Mother Frost. She did her work very well and Mother Frost was very pleased with her. Then one day the step-daughter said,

'Mother Frost, I'd like to go home.'

So Mother Frost said, 'You've worked so hard that I'll show you the way myself.'

She led her to a big gateway. As the step-daughter walked through it a shower of gold fell on her. It covered her from head to foot. It made her more beautiful than ever.

`This is your reward for having worked so well,' said Mother Frost returning her spindle. Then the step-daughter found herself in her own garden.

The Cock saw her and crowed,

`Cock-a-doodle doo!

Our golden lady has come home too!

For you're only paid for what you do!'

The step-mother was so surprised and pleased that she began treating her well. Then she heard her story and sent her own daughter to the river.

Her daughter threw her spindle into the river and jumped in after it. She, too, found herself in a beautiful green meadow. Soon she came to the apple tree.

`Shake me! Shake me!' cried the tree.

`Why should I ?' said the girl rudely and walked on.

Soon she came to the oven with the cakes.

`Take us out! Take us out!' cried the cakes.

`Why should I? said the girl rudely and walked on.

Now she came to the house of Mother Frost.

`Would you like me to work for you?' she asked Mother Frost.

`Yes, I would,' said Mother Frost. 'But you must take care to make my bed well. Shake it so that the feathers fly about. Then children on earth will say that it's snowing. For you know, ...'

`Yes, I know you're Mother Frost,' said the girl.

So the girl began working for Mother Frost. For two days she worked well but by the third day she was back to her lazy ways. Till finally Mother Frost said, 'It's time for you to go home.'

The girl was very pleased. This is what she wanted. Mother Frost led her to the gateway. As she passed through it a bucket of pitch fell on her and covered her from head to foot. It made her uglier than ever. 'This is your reward for being lazy,' said Mother Frost returning her spindle. Then the the lazy daughter found herself in her own garden.

The Cock saw her and crowed,'

`Cock-a-doodle-doo!

Our Sticky Lady has come home too!

For you're only paid for what you do!'

3. Two Out Of The Bag

Once upon a time there lived, near a forest, an old man and an old woman. The old man used to set traps for animals. Whenever an animal was caught, the old woman would make a very fine dinner. But the day no animal was caught, the old woman would scold the old man and sometimes, I'm sorry to say, would beat him with her broom.

One day the old man saw that he had trapped a crane. He was very pleased. But the Crane said, `Old man, if you let me go, I'll give you a magic bag so that you're never hungry again.'

So the old man set the Crane free and the Crane gave him a bag. 'Whenever you are hungry, say, Two out of the Bag!' When food appears, eat and then say, 'Two into the Bag!'

Then the Crane flew away. The old man said, Two out of the Bag!' At once two little black boys came out of the bag. They brought out a table, spread on it a white cloth and placed on it dishes and dishes of the tastiest food he had ever seen. The old man ate and ate. When he had finished he said, Two into the Bag!'

Quick as a wink, everything disappeared into the bag.

Now the old man went on his way. He came to a poor wood-cutter's cottage. There lived his wife and three daughters. They were very hungry. So the old man said, 'I'll get you something to eat.

He placed his bag on the ground and said, Two out of the Bag!'

At once the little black boys brought out delicious food. The wood-cutter's wife and his daughters couldn't believe their eyes. They ate until they could eat no more. Then the old man said, 'Two into the Bag!' and just as before everything disappeared.

Now the wood-cutter's wife decided to take away the magic bag. So she took the old man out into the garden while her daughters quickly sewed another bag just like the magic bag and replaced it.

The old man did not know that his bag had been changed. He took the new bag and went home. He said to his wife, 'I'll give you something nice to eat. I have a magic bag.' He placed the bag on the ground and said, 'Two out of the Bag!'

But nothing happened. The old woman was so angry that she beat the old man harder than ever.

So the next morning the old man called out to the Crane. It came at once. He told him what had happened.

`The wood-cutter's wife must have changed your bag,' said the Crane. 'I'll give you another bag. If you use it wisely you'll get your first bag back.'

The Crane dropped another bag at his feet and flew off. - The old man said, `Two out of the Bag!' At once two little black boys came out and began beating him with sticks.

The old man was very surprised. 'Stop!' he cried. 'Stop!' but the boys didn't stop. Then he said, `Two into the Bag!' Quick as a wink, the boys disappeared into the bag. Now the old man took the bag and went to the wood-cutter's cottage. He said, 'I have a bag even more wonderful than the first.'

Then he went into the garden. Quickly the daughters sewed another bag and replaced the magic bag. Then they said, Two out of the Bag!'

At once the two black boys came out and began to beat the old woman and her daughters.

`Stop!' they begged, 'Please, stop!'

But the black boys went on beating them. The wood-cutter's wife said, 'Please, old man make them stop. You can have your first bag back.'

So the old man said, Two into the Bag!' The black boys disappeared and the woman returned the first bag. The old man took the bags and went home. His wife was waiting.

`This is the bag I told you about.' said the old man giving her the second bag. The old woman said. Two out of the Bag!' At once the two black boys came out and began to beat her. The old woman was so surprised that she fell over backwards.

`Save me, old man!' she cried.

So the old man said, `Two into the Bag!'

At once the two black boys disappeared. Now the old man took the first bag and said, `Two out of the Bag!'

At once the two black boys brought out delicious food.

`Let's eat,' said the old man. So they had a very fine dinner. The old woman was so pleased that she never again beat the old man or even scolded him.

They lived happily ever after.

4. The Pied Piper

Once upon a time the town of Hamelin in Germany was terribly troubled by a whole army of rats. There were rats of all shapes, sizes and colours. They used to eat all the food grains, nibble all the clothes and didn't even spare the wood of furniture. They were fearless, they were numerous, they were terrible! The people didn't know what to do about them. They thought of various methods to get rid of the rats but each one of them failed. The people were so upset that they even thought of leaving Hamelin.

But then there came a strange man to Hamelin. He was tall and thin. He wore a long, colourful coat and a large hat. His face was thin. He had a long nose and crooked teeth. He had a pipe hanging round his neck. He came up to the Mayor and said, 'I am the Pied Piper. I can get rid of the army of rats for you.

The Mayor was delighted. `Oh, please do,' he said. 'We are sick and tired of these rats. We really don't know what to do!'

`Don't worry,' said the strange man. 'I know what to do. I'll get you rid of these rats. But you must give me a hundred pieces of gold.'

`Oh please! Please take a hundred pieces of gold but get rid of these rats for us!' cried the Mayor.

So the Pied Piper stepped out. He put the flute to his lips and began to play. It was a strange sound : nothing like anyone had ever heard before. At the very first notes - what did the people see? Rats! Rats rushing out from wherever they had been hiding. There were so many of them! Hundreds! Thousands! And all of them went rushing out behind the Pied Piper. They followed him as if they were under a spell. The people watched in amazement. Never had they seen such a sight! They watched as the Pied Piper led them to the river. They hardly dared to breathe as the Piper stepped into the river. They held their breaths as the rats followed him into the river one by one until the whole army of rats was drowned. How the people cheered! How happy they were!

The Pied Piper walked back and went to the Mayor. 'I have done as you asked,' he said. 'Now give me my hundred pieces of gold.'

`A hundred pieces of gold!' cried the Mayor. 'What do you want a hundred pieces of gold for? Here, take a hundred pieces of silver.'

`Don't break your promise,' said the Pied Piper.

`What promise?' shouted the Mayor. 'Take these pieces of silver and get lost! Who on earth would give a hundred pieces of gold to a beggar like you?'

`Well,' said the Pied Piper quietly. 'Don't say I didn't warn you.'

`We're not afraid of you,' said the Mayor and the people. The rats are dead. They cannot come back to life.'

The Pied Piper said never a word. He put the flute to his lips.

The people laughed. 'This crazy Pied Piper cannot do anything!' they said.

As the first notes were heard - all the children of Hamelin -all the boys and girls, chubby-cheeked and thin, golden-haired and dark haired, blue-eyed and brown-eyed, ran out leaving aside whatever they had been doing. The Piper began to walk down the path to the river and the children followed laughing and chattering. The people were shocked. Some of them were too surprised to react - others who tried to stop the children found that none of the children listened. They followed the Pied Piper as if under a spell.

The people watched in dismay. Would he drown their children too? But, no, as they came to the river, the Pied Piper turned and began to walk on the path that led away from the river and to the mountain. He kept on playing the strange, high notes and the children kept on following him. Now the people were relieved.

` Our children cannot climb the mountain,' they said. 'They'll be safe.'

But when they reached the mountain lo and behold! A door suddenly opened in the mountain-side and the Pied Piper walked through the door and disappeared into the mountain. The children went after the Pied Piper one by one and they too disappeared. The door closed and then the door too vanished! All the children of Hamelin had gone!

The people of Hamelin were filled with sorrow. They never saw the Pied Piper or their children again. Hamelin became a sad, quiet town. The people never smiled. They never forgot the terrible price they had paid for breaking their promise.

5. The Four Friends

Once upon a time there lived a man with a donkey. Now this donkey had become old and was unable to work. So his master chased the donkey out of the house.

The donkey walked along slowly and sadly. Alas!' he said to himself. 'Where will I live? What will I eat?' Then a sudden thought struck him. 'I know what I'll do!' he said. 'I'll go to Bremen town and join the band there. I sing so well. How happy everyone will be to hear me sing!'

So he began to trot happily towards Bremen. Just then he saw a dog. It was sitting by the side of the road and whining. The donkey stopped at once.

`Why are you crying, Brother Dog?' he asked.

The dog sadly replied, 'When I was young, I used to guard my master's house. Now I've become old, so my master has thrown me out.'

Well,' said the donkey. `I'm going to Bremen to join the band. Why don't you come along with me?'

The dog readily agreed. The two friends walked along. They had not gone far when they met a cat. She was sitting sadly by the roadside.

`Why are you so sad, Mistress Puss?' asked the donkey.

The cat replied sadly, 'When I was young I used to keep my master's house free of mice. Now that I've become old my master has shown me the door.'

`Well, that's no problem,' said the donkey. `We're going to Bremen to join the band. Why don't you come along with us?'

The cat readily agreed. The three friends walked along happily. They now met a rooster. He was sitting on a stile and crowing loudly.

`What are you crowing so loudly for?' asked the donkey.

`My master is planning to kill me and cook me for tomorrow's dinner,' said the rooster. `So I'm crowing while I may.'

Well,' said the donkey. 'There's no need to become anyone's dinner. Come with us to Bremen and we'll join the band.'

The rooster was only too happy to go with the other three. Now the four friends walked happily towards Bremen. Their way lay through a forest. Hardly had they entered the forest when night fell. Just then they saw a light.

`Let's ask the people who live here if we can spend the night,' said the donkey.

So they went to the house and peeped in. And what did they .see? They saw four men seated at a table. They were robbers. But the four animals had eyes only for the food - chicken and meat, milk and cheese, salad and cream, fruit and vegetables and so much more!

By now everyone's mouth was watering. 'I'll tell you what,! said the

donkey. 'Let's sing. Then these people will be so happy that they'll call us in for dinner.'

So they all began to sing - the donkey brayed, the dog barked, the cat mewed, the rooster crowed and there was such a lot of noise that the robbers thought there were witches and ghosts in the house. They jumped up and ran out of the house.

`Look!' cried the donkey. 'They have left the meal for us!' So the four friends went inside and had ,the tastiest meal they had ever eaten. They now started feeling sleepy. So each chose the place he liked the best. The donkey lay down in the yard, the dog by the door, the cat in the warm ashes of the fire-place and the cock chose the roof-top. Soon they were fast asleep.

Meanwhile the robbers were feeling rather ashamed of themselves for having left their house in such a hurry.

`We're robbers,' said their leader. 'We shouldn't have run away.' Then he turned to one of his men. 'Go and see whether everything is fine there,' he said.

So the bravest robber went back to the house. Quietly, he opened the gate. Softly, he opened the front door. There was not a sound. The animals kept sleeping peacefully. Then he came to the fire-place. The cat opened her eyes and looked at him sleepily. The robber saw the cat's eyes shining. He thought that they were glowing coals. So he put out his hand to light a match. Immediately the cat scratched his face. He gave a howl of fright and pain and rushed to the door.

He almost stumbled over the dog who was so surprised that he bit him in the leg. The robber gave a loud yell and rushed out. He ran straight into the donkey who immediately kicked him. The robber yelled as loudly as he could. The cock was awakened by all this noise and started crowing loudly, 'Cock-a-doodle doo! Cock-a-doodle-doo!'

The robber ran without stopping till he reached his friends. His friends were shocked to see him bruised, bleeding and terribly frightened. When the robber was finally able to speak, he said, 'I entered the house quietly. However, when I reached the kitchen and tried to light a match from the glowing coals, a witch flew at me and scratched my face. When I rushed out, a goblin flew at me and stabbed me in the leg with his knife. Hardly had I got to the yard when a giant hit me with his club. As I ran, I heard the goblin on the roof. He was shouting, 'Cut his neck off, too! Cut his neck off, too!'

This scared the robbers so much that they decided never to go to that house again. As for the four friends, they liked the place so much that they decided not to go to Bremen after all but live there. And if you'd like to see them, that's exactly where you'll find them!

6. Puss-in-Boots I

Once there lived a farmer. When he was about to die, he gave his eldest son all his land, his second son all his cattle and his third son - his cat.

Now Jack (for that was the third son's name) sat under a tree wondering what to do. Just then he heard a voice say, 'Well, Jack, get to work.'

Jack looked around. There was no one to be seen. 'Who spoke?' asked Jack.

'I did,' said the cat.

'You!' cried Jack. 'But I've never heard a cat speak!'

'I'm not an ordinary cat,' said the cat proudly. 'Now go and get me a suit of clothes, a hat and big leather boots to wear.'

'To wear!' repeated Jack in surprise. 'But I've never seen a cat wearing clothes or boots!'

'Look, Jack,' said the cat sternly. 'There's a lot you haven't heard or seen. Just do as I ask.'

So Jack did as the cat asked. When the cat wore the suit of clothes, the hat and the big leather boots - she really looked something out of a story-book.

'How smart you look!' said Jack.

Thank-you, Jack.' said the cat. 'From now on you may call me Puss-in-Boots.

' Next morning Puss-in-Boots carefully laid some traps. Soon she trapped a pair of pigeons. She carefully wrapped them up and went to the king's palace.

'I want to see the king,' said Puss-in-Boots.

The soldiers were very surprised to hear a cat speak but they said, 'The king is busy. You can't see him.'

Puss-in-Boots looked at them coldly. 'Have you ever heard or seen a cat that talked? You haven't? I thought not. Now if you know what's good for you, you'd better do as I ask.'

So the soldiers let her in. The king stared in surprise. He'd never seen such a splendid cat. She bowed low before the king and said, 'Prince Jack has sent this gift for you.' Then she handed him the pigeons.

The king had never heard of a prince called Jack but didn't like to say so. So he said, 'Thank him for me.'

The next morning Puss-in-Boots trapped a pair of rabbits. Then off she went to the King's palace. This time no one stopped her and she was admitted at once into the king's presence. She bowed low before the king and said, 'Prince Jack has sent this gift for you.

The king smiled. Another gift? Thank him for me.'

Now Puss-in-Boots kept on taking gifts for the king for a few days. Sometimes it was the fruit she stole from orchards, sometimes it was the animals she trapped. By now the king was very impressed. He said, 'I'd very much like to meet Prince Jack.'

`Well,' said Puss-in-Boots airily. 'I don't know when that would be possible. Prince Jack is always busy looking after his lands and properties.'

` I'd like to meet him whenever he has the time,' said the king.

The next morning Puss took Jack to the river where the king and his daughter went driving every morning. 'It's time for you have a bath,' she said to Jack.

So Jack took off his clothes and dived into the river. Puss hid Jack's clothes and waited by the bushes. As soon as she saw the king's carriage coming, she shouted, 'Help! Robbers! Help!'

The king stopped the carriage. 'What's the matter, Puss-in-Boots?' he asked.

`Robbers have made away with Prince Jack's clothes and jewels,' cried Puss-in-Boots. 'And poor Prince Jack is still swimming in the river.'

`Don't worry,' said the king. He sent his soldiers to get a suit of his own rich clothes and a set of the finest jewels for Jack.

Let Prince Jack dress,' said the king. 'I'll wait for him. Perhaps he'll ride with me?'

Jack was amazed to see the beautiful clothes and jewels but did as Puss-in-Boots said and wore them. When he came out in front of the king, he really looked like a handsome prince. The king's daughter had never seen such a handsome young man. She fell in love with him.

The king invited Jack to ride with him. As soon as Jack was seated, Puss said, 'Your Majesty, you're invited to lunch at our castle. Just follow this road, please. I'll walk on ahead and ask the servants to get lunch ready.'

— 7. Puss-in-Boots II —

The king's carriage rolled slowly down the road while Puss ran on ahead. She soon came to a stretch of green fields. `Whose fields are these?' she asked.

`They belong to Gogia the Giant,' said the workers.

`Well now they don't,' said Puss-in-Boots. 'They belong to Prince Jack. And if you know what's good for you you'd better say so, too.'

The workers were too frightened to refuse.

Puss walked on. Now she came to a stretch of orchards. The orchards were full of fruit trees laden with fruit. Puss asked `Whose orchards are these?'

`They belong to Gogia the Giant,' said the workers.

`Well, now they don't,' said Puss- in-Boots. 'They belong to Prince Jack. And if you know what's good for you, you'd better say so, too.'

The workers were too frightened to refuse.

Puss walked on. Now she came to a huge castle. It had four grey walls and four grey towers and was surrounded by the most beautiful garden that Puss had ever seen. Puss walked in. 'Whose castle is this?' asked Puss-in-Boots.

`It belongs to Gogia the Giant,' said a servant. Just then Puss heard a voice like thunder. 'It belongs to ME, Puss!' said a loud voice behind Puss. 'For I am Gogia the Giant,'

Puss-in-Boots turned. And she saw the biggest giant she had ever seen. His eyes were like dinner plates and his legs like tree-trunks! He seemed to be touch the roof.

Puss was frightened but said, 'Oh, Gogia the Giant! And what can YOU do?'

'A number of things,' said the Giant. 'I can turn myself into anything I wish,' and he turned himself into a huge lion.

`Oh, my goodness!' cried Puss-in-Boots and sprang to the top of the mantlepiece. 'That was easy!' she cried. 'Because you yourself are so huge. Now let's see if you can turn yourself into something small like ..... say a mouse!'

So the giant turned himself into a mouse. Quick as a wink, Puss caught him and ate him up!

Then she came out and told the servants, 'You have a new master. Hurry up and prepare the finest meal you can. He'll soon be here.'

Meanwhile the king's carriage drove by the green fields. `Whose fields are these?' asked the king.

`They belong to Prince Jack,' said the workers.

The king was impressed.

Now they drove by the orchards. 'Whose orchard are these?' asked the king.

`They belong to Prince Jack,' said the workers.

The king was very impressed.

Now they came to the castle. The king and his daughter gazed in wonder at the beautiful garden and the huge castle. The servants, led by Puss-in-Boots, came out and bowed low.

`You're welcome to Prince Jack's castle, Your Majesty,' they said.

Now the king was even more impressed. Then he was served the finest meal he'd ever tasted. The king was so pleased with Jack's riches, his good looks and his simple friendly nature that he got his daughter married to him.

So Jack, the princess and Puss-in-Boots lived happily ever after.